S u c c

Small Gardens

MARIANNE SCHEU-HELGERT

Series Editor:
LESLEY YOUNG

MEREHURST

Introduction

Even the smallest patch of garden can be transformed into a green oasis. No matter whether you own a pocket-handkerchief-sized garden, a tiny, perhaps irregularly shaped, plot or a paved courtyard, this guide will provide all the help you require for the successful designing and planning of a small garden. Problems that may be hardly noticeable in a larger garden show up instantly in a small garden – for example, planning mistakes and the wrong choice of plants. The first step towards success, therefore, is to be absolutely clear about what you are trying to achieve.

In this book, expert gardener Marianne Scheu-Helgert offers sensible advice on how to tackle important decisions and there are also step-by-step illustrations showing you how to plan and build paths, steps, walls, fences, garden nooks, pergolas and ponds in small gardens. You will also find enchanting ideas for attractive designs using plants. The illustrations cover all the practical tasks you may wish to try, while glorious colour photographs prove that it is not at all difficult to turn a small garden into a veritable paradise.

Contents

A small garden containing everything your heart could desire.

Space-saving climbers: Clematis (left) and nasturtium (right).

The author

Having trained as a gardener, Marianne Scheu-Helgert studied garden design at the Technical University of Munich-Weihenstephan. She now heads the department of information at the Bavarian Federal Institute for wine growing and gardening in Veitshochheim, Germany.

The photographers

Ulrike Schneiders studied photography at the Bayerische Staatslehranstalt für Fotographie and also with her father Toni Schneiders. She now works for many calendar and art publishing companies. Jürgen Becker studied art and, for the last twelve years, has worked as a photographer for book and calendar publishing companies as well as for international newspapers and periodicals.

The illustrator

György Jankovics studied art and graphic design in Budapest and Hamburg. He has produced plant and animal studies for a number of well-known publishing houses and has illustrated numerous volumes in the "Success with ..." gardening series.

NB: Please read the Author's Notes on page 61 so that your enjoyment of your garden may remain unimpaired.

The ideal garden

"What can I do with such a small garden?" is a common question among those who would like to redesign their garden. The first step is to make a complete list of both existing conditions and your own wishes. The following pages will provide everything you need to know to embark on this new venture with confidence.

Left: Ugly walls can be disguised with climbing roses.
Top: Walls may even disappear behind espaliers. Here an espalier and a mirror create the illusion of a path and the view of another garden beyond.

The ideal garden

Getting to know your garden

Gardens are pockets of "redesigned" nature. In recognizing this, it is a good idea to alter the natural conditions found in your garden as little as possible. Drastic interference, for example, attempting to create a heather garden in unsuitable soil, will create a lot of work initially and, later on, a great deal of continuous time and care. The key conditions to consider right from the start include:

Soil: The best garden soil is loose, humus-rich, slightly loamy and slightly sandy. Suitable plants can also be obtained for very poor soils, such as very sandy or marshy ones. If you have not yet got to know your garden soil, it is a good idea to have it analysed by sending a couple of soil samples to a laboratory which offers this service (ask at your local garden centre). You can also buy a DIY soil analysis kit which will tell you how to extract samples and will provide advice on soil improvement. Soils in the gardens of newly built houses, which have usually become compacted through the use of heavy machinery on the site, will create particular difficulties in the early years. Advice on what to do in such circumstances is given on pages 30 and 31.

Light: Most garden owners looking for a place to relax will appreciate a spot in the sun. When planning your garden, therefore, remember that while the sun always moves in a large, high arc across the sky from east to west, in winter this arc becomes much shorter and is lower in the sky. Make a sketch of your garden, including all buildings and trees that create shadows, and mark the positions lit by the morning sun in midsummer or late in the evening and where you might find a cool spot in the shade at midday.

Noise and wind: If you wish to build a nook for a garden seat, it is a good idea to plan some protection from noise or wind on the side where such nuisances enter the garden. Plan in features such as thick hedges, wooden fences or walls.

Creating a new design or redesigning

In the case of a completely new design, planning the garden should begin even before the house is built. If the building is to be set well back from the road, you will end up with a large front garden. If you save on frontage, you will gain extra space in your back garden.

If you are planning to redesign an existing garden, try to integrate any treasures that you have inherited.

● Do not thoughtlessly fell older, healthy trees. They may create shadows but they also provide a certain atmosphere that will take many years to reproduce. Always plant a young tree as soon as possible to replace a diseased, old tree that has had to be cut down.

● Elderly deciduous hedges or espalier trees can often be rejuvenated by cutting out old wood.

● If you need to take out ancient fruit trees or rose bushes, you can often obtain valuable old varieties that have been grafted on to new stocks.

● Try to salvage old climbing plants. Carefully remove them from the wall while rebuilding or renovating work is done on the wall. Even the odd preserved shoot will create a new green curtain within a few weeks.

● Retain vegetable beds as they are usually particularly fertile after years of composting or manuring. You can continue to use such areas for growing vegetables or for nutrient-hungry plantings such as perennials, soft fruit, espalier fruit, roses and summer flowers. Undemanding plants, a flower lawn or an alpine collection will not thrive on this type of soil.

● If possible, try to retain paths, steps, walls, fences or posts made of natural stone as these materials are almost indestructible, while artificial replacements are generally not so durable.

A sitting area and a small vegetable garden can be integrated in a very small space.

Working out what you want

You will soon realize that, in a really small garden, not all of the things you would like to do can actually be done. You may have to be realistic and set limits for yourself. Pursue one, two or even three of your most important goals and leave the rest. Some of your other ambitions could be achieved in other ways or by making clever use of empty corners. If your most important requirements are a place to sit, a grassy play area and a vegetable garden, then plan these generously. Your other wishes should be secondary to these.

A shrubbery or fruit trees can be planted in strips to form boundaries between three such different areas of the garden. The garden pond you have always dreamed of may be translated into a water trough surrounded by plants beside a garden seat. A lawn used as a play area may also be used for sunbathing, while a screen of espalier fruit trees will provide privacy.

The ideal garden

Decide what you want

Feature	What to consider	Alternatives
A flowering hedge	Will require a lot of space, up to 3 m (10 ft) wide.	Climbing plants or tall flowering plants along a fence.
A flowering lawn	Only effective in a large area. Should not be walked on much. Needs to be mown twice a year with a scythe.	A robust lawn. If you still want flowers, plan a bed with simple summer flowers or a wild flower mixture.
Trees	Keep at a good distance from neighbouring boundary. Create shadow! Deciduous trees look nice but drop leaves in autumn. Conifers are evergreen, not much work but fairly boring.	Choose low-growing trees or bushes.
Enclosure	Wall, fence, trimmed or untrimmed hedge. Keep hedge as low as possible in small gardens.	Shrubs or thorny hedges without a fence. Discuss with neighbours a communal shrub border, a group of small trees or path instead of enclosure.
A green façade	● Climbing plants need a climbing aid. ● Grow climbers with suckers only on façades that will not be damaged.	● Sow new annual climbers every year. ● Plant espalier fruit 50 cm (20 in) from the façade.
A bower	Site well away from the house. Open-sided or enclosed structure.	Install a garden seat instead, possibly in a lean-to beside a building.
Vegetables	Require sunny, sheltered position, humus-rich soil. Take a lot of time and work.	Grow vegetables in large containers and boxes or between flowers and herbs.
Tool store	In a cellar, garage, shed. Direct access to garden is useful.	Weather-hardy tool chest on a patio or in the garden.
Composting station	Choose not very visible, sheltered position. Sufficient space for turning etc.	Install a small, commercially produced composting bin.
Herbs	Fully sunny position. Cultivate annual herbs separately from perennial ones.	Grow in pots/large containers or among ornamental plants and vegetables.
Protection from noise	Particularly effective: walls or thick hedges, fences with dense greenery.	Try massive wooden fences though not quite as effective.
Walls	● To enclose an area: find out if planning permission is required. ● As a support on slopes etc.: walls made of natural stone are attractive but expensive.	● Wooden structures can also create boundaries and visual screens. ● Wooden palisades are an alternative to support slopes.

Feature	What to consider	Alternatives
Fruit	● Fruit trees, gooseberries and strawberries require a sunny position. ● Currants, blackberries and raspberries will cope with periods of shade throughout the day. ● Fruit trees will not require much space if they are planted along paths or driveways. ● Choose robust varieties.	Further space-saving ideas: ● Pyramid-shaped trees on an espalier are suitable for fencing off areas of the garden. ● Small standard apple trees and soft fruit bushes can be grown in large containers. ● Climbing strawberries can be grown in hanging containers or trained up climbing frames.
Pergola	● Obtainable as kits. ● Suitable for sitting area, storage area or in front of an entrance.	A construction based on your own plans. Wires can be used to support the inner sections.
Roses	Fully sunny position. Choose robust varieties or frequent spraying will be necessary.	Instead, use flowering shrubs, flowering climbers or summer flowers.
Trimmed hedge	Requires 1-1.5 m (40-60 in) width. Keep at least 50 cm (20 in) distance from neighbouring property.	A fence with flowers or a fruit espalier.
Visual screen	Hedges of evergreen woody species, a pergola covered in climbers, a solid wooden fence.	Various types of shade during the summer; blackberries on an espalier.
Sitting area	Main area for a seat/barbecue site near house, area as sunny as possible.	A second sitting area with different lighting conditions.
Area for play	Sand tray, swing, seesaw, tree house, lawned play area in an easily supervised position, particularly from kitchen window.	Possibilities for children to play on the patio or in a storage area.
Pond	Sunny position, not underneath deciduous trees or falling leaves will pollute the pondwater. NB: make the area safe for children, including children not belonging to your household!	Water troughs, bird baths, fountains.
Outside tap	Good for a detached house: install taps on opposite sides of the house.	Waterbutts connected to gutters.
Paths	Main path should be at least 1.2 m (48 in) wide; other paths 60-80 cm (24-32 in) wide.	Stepping stones across lawn or between shrubs instead of proper paths.
Fences	Choose a design that complements the style of the house and the environment; keep it as low as possible.	Hedges, thorny bushes or taller plantings.

The ideal garden

Climbing roses on an espalier and two small trees in pots beside the door.

Small children in the garden

Families with a baby should delay installing certain features until the child has grown. Consider the following points when planning.

● A flowering "meadow" is not suitable as a play area as it should not be walked on until after the main flowering time is over and the grass has been mown down in early summer.

● A garden pond can become a death trap for a small child even if it is only about 10 cm (4 in) deep. The best plan is not to build a pond until your children are bigger. Even safety precautions such as a solid fence or grid installed just below the surface of the water cannot prevent all accidents!

● Rare plants are generally demanding and will require a lot of care. If you want to spend more of your leisure time with your family you should choose robust, easy-to-care-for plants.

● Once the children are older, plans for various features can be considered again. The play area could be turned into a vegetable patch and a rockery could take over the space once occupied by a sand tray. Special features, such as a rose garden, can now become reality.

Front gardens

The area in front of the house is used as a reception area, entrance drive, parking area for a car, pram, bicycle or dustbin and, above all, as a place for a chat with neighbours. Try to consider the following points so that your front garden may meet all these requirements.

Electricity: If you are planning a completely new front garden, you should install any cable systems required for lighting, automatic door openers, etc. before the topsoil is put in place. Adequate lighting at the entrance door, garage and along paths improves safety, creates a welcoming effect for visitors and will deter potential burglars.

Boundaries: These should keep strangers and animals out of your property. Of course, if you have a good rapport with your neighbours you might not need a fence between the properties, however, various possibilities for a boundary to the road or street can be considered.

● A planted boundary about 50 cm (20 in) in height; for example, of prickly, ground-covering roses, will be sufficient to prevent small children from running out into the road.

● If you prefer a fence, you should aim for a simple design

that blends in well and looks neat.

● Hedges make natural visual, wind, noise and dust screens. Reckon on a width of 1 m (40 in) for trimmed hedges comprising either deciduous or coniferous species. A hedge of untrimmed flowering shrubs will require about 2.5 m (8 ft) width. Small front gardens with thick, tall hedges will appear even smaller.

Paths: You need not pave over the entire area in front of the house. It will be sufficient to reinforce the most frequented sections of path; that is, from the front door to the garage and to the gate. This will also have the great advantage of cutting down on the amount of dirt carried into the house.

The house entrance: This is the first impression that visitors receive. I recommend an attractive paving of natural stone or frost-proof bricks. Large container plants, climbing plants or a seat look very inviting beside a front door

Driveway to garage and storage area: If possible, avoid a tarmac surface. A more natural-looking design is created by a gravelled area with concreted strips for the car wheels.

Drain covers: These are least conspicuous when set in solidly reinforced areas or between tall plantings.

Dustbins: Hide these in an easily accessible place between a fence and hedge or behind a foliage-covered climbing frame.

You will also save more room if you install an expensive, although often very ugly, dustbin cubicle. The standing surface for dustbins should definitely be tarmac or paved.

A tree near the house: This will visually enlarge the garden, particularly if a small-growing species with delicate foliage is chosen. Fruit trees are also suitable. A deciduous tree providing shade across paths in the summer is very pleasant. It may also create a harmonious transition from a storage area to the garden proper. Trees such as an ornamental cherry (*Prunus serrulata*) are extremely attractive.

The ideal garden

Small courtyards can be made appealing with plants in containers.

Containers and a painted gate bring colour to a garden courtyard.

Gardens of terraced houses

Long, narrow gardens can be divided up into several different areas.

● A sitting area beside a house may be furnished with greenery and framed with a green trellis covered in climbing plants, a pergola, a flowering hedge, a rose espalier or a planting of tall perennials.

● Behind this feature there might be room for a lawned area or a bed for flowers, for a vegetable patch, a pond, or a shrubbery. Again, the area can be framed in various ways, with plants all around the periphery and along the footpath.

● In the case of very long, narrow gardens, there may even be space for a third area or, at the very least, room for a further area for sitting in.

My tip: Families with children will find it a great advantage to have a boundary fence, at least in the back garden. If neighbours agree, there could even be space for a shared adventure playground for all the children in the terrace, with trees for climbing and a hut.

Gardens around a block of flats

In some such buildings a separate parcel of land is retained by each flat owner for their own private use. Often, however, fences have been dispensed with between these plots, although a communal, low fence or hedge can be a sensible solution along the side bordering a road or street. A friendly atmosphere can be encouraged among the inhabitants of the building by means of a communal sitting area.

Back gardens

These can be turned into lush, green gardens if you plant flowers, climbing plants and shrubs in beds along the housewalls. A sitting area combined with a play area, or at least a sand tray with a cover, can provide good conditions for friendly social mingling of older and younger members of a family. The ground may be covered with paving slabs or stones set so that grass will grow up through the cracks to provide a little extra greenery.

Legal matters

All householders and tenants must observe building regulations, tenancy agreements and the law when planning a garden or making changes to an existing garden. It will be necessary to apply for planning permission before erecting any constructions or permanent fixtures. It is also important to take into account your neighbours' rights to privacy,

peace and quiet and light. If in doubt, consult your local council or a solicitor.

Minimum distances from boundaries: Think carefully before planting trees near a neighbouring boundary. You will probably require your neighbours' consent before you can erect any large structure such as a pergola or even a wall if this is going to obstruct your neighbours' light. Also make certain that any large trees or building work will not cause damage to the foundations of your neighbours' property or alter their drainage arrangements. Remember that trees can grow very tall over the years and can become a storm hazard if too close to buildings. They also drop leaves and fruit in autumn and can prove a real nuisance and expense for your neighbours.

My tip: Avoid disagreements by showing considerate behaviour. Always discuss any planting that will lead to tall mature growth with your neighbour. Your trees or hedges might one day cut off light from your neighbour's living room or garden even if you keep to a reasonable minimum distance from a boundary.

Fences and walls: Again, before building these, discuss your plans with your neighbour. You will have to maintain all fences and walls on your own property but if the structures are on the boundary, your neighbours may be responsible for their care.

Emissions: Odours, noise and

falling leaves from a neighbour's garden have to be put up with if they only superficially interfere with your use of your own garden, are a "local feature", and cannot be avoided using normal economic measures.

Roots and branches: If these intrude into your own garden from a neighbouring one, you may ask for them to be removed within a certain period of time if the use of your own garden is impaired by the intrusion. If your neighbour allows the stipulated time to pass without doing anything to remedy the situation, you are permitted to remove branches or roots in a proper manner.

Fallen fruit: If fruit drops from a neighbouring tree on to your property, you can ask them to come and remove it or allow you to dispose of it as you wish. If fruit drops on to a public area (a pavement, for example), it will still belong to the owner of the tree. In the case of accidents (someone slipping on fruit), this may lead to legal repercussions.

Tree protection regulations: In many parishes, older trees may only be felled, sawn or have their roots exposed after obtaining permission. Consult your local council.

Ownership: When you move house, you should stipulate to the buyers of your property which, if any, plants you intend to take with you as they are, legally, fixtures on the property.

Planning and building

If you are planning a new garden or a total change of design, you must proceed step by step. The following pages will tell you what needs to be considered, from the first sketch right through to the final planting.

Left: A sitting area has been created in the middle of greenery under an elegant sunshade beside a small pond. There is an attractive framework of flowers and shrubs and, a little to one side, a barbecue area for summer parties with friends.
Top: A plant for moist, marginal areas. The yellow iris (Iris pseudacorus) feels particularly at home at the edge of a pond.

Planning and building

The important elements in a garden

Thorough initial planning will avoid mistakes and unnecessary work. In particular, measures that involve large-scale earth movement should be carefully considered beforehand.

● Gardens on a slope need not be completely terraced with high supporting walls. Only the sitting area, the play area or a pond require level surfaces. Most other garden elements are possible even on a slope.

● On flat terrain, on the other hand, gentle, artificial mounds may gain you extra space.

● Tall plants, hedges, plants growing on free-standing climbing aids or fruit espaliers make good spatial dividers.

● A visual screen near the side of the garden that borders on a road or some other public area can be erected to give privacy to a nook to sit in. The other sides can be loosely covered in greenery so that there is still a view.

● Windows and doors along a housewall should not be obscured with plants. They must be able to let in light and also provide pleasant views.

● Generous views through plants will connect the various garden elements visually with each other.

● Bodies of water in a garden will improve the mini-climate, particularly near a sitting area.

● Lawned play areas or ornamental lawns require intensive soil preparation and care. A general-purpose lawn is easier to look after. A flowering "meadow" should not be situated right beside a splendid shrubbery or summer flowerbeds as these areas will spoil the attraction of each other.

● Such necessary items as a bicycle or car parking area, dustbins, a composting station or a tool shed can be harmoniously blended with the other garden elements.

Building elements

Paving slabs or natural stone are most suitable for a sitting area near the house. Cement paving slabs are cheaper but it is worth choosing simple shapes and inconspicuous colours and combining two different types of material.

Paths: One type of stone or slabs should be utilized for all most frequented paths. Gravel paths will do for the back of the garden. The garden will appear larger if you allow the edges of the paths to become slightly overgrown with plants.

Steps: Steps should be spaced for the average adult footstep (see pp. 20/21). Use material that is inconspicuous and blends well with the paths.

Walls: These should be no taller nor more massive than absolutely necessary. They will appear less stark if they have plants growing beside or over them and are used around a sitting area.

Fences: The best materials for low, semi-transparent boundaries are simple wooden battens without a visually limiting fence base. If you wish, however, you can still equip the fence with a foundation strip along the ground.

Pergola: The best types are made of wood and will require a width of about 50 cm (20 in).

Hedge: A hedge planted along a small wall offers particularly good protection against noise, dust and lack of privacy.

Ponds: Premoulded, ready-to-fit ponds can be obtained in the trade. These are then just sunk into the ground. You could also create a miniature pond in a waterproof vessel on a patio or in the garden. Slopes even present the possibility of building a little stream and waterfall.
Individually formed ponds using flexible liner have to be built on even ground and only look good with a wide strip of plants around the edge. They therefore need a lot of room.

Play area: A sand tray made of wood does not require much room. If you have more space you can even set up apparatus such as a swing.

Terraces: If your garden is on a slope, the entrances to the property, house and garden should be visually integrated. The broader the terraces are on a slope, the higher the supporting walls and verges will need to be and they will create very clear divisions. Terraced steps creating distinct areas of garden can be most attractive. The less room you set aside for a sitting area near the house, the more room will be available somewhere else for a lawn seat or sunbathing.

Instead of tall, expensive walls you can build several low drystone walls yourself (see pp. 20/21). All in all, this will create a more spacious and less conspicuous effect. Try planning in a flowering "meadow", a rockery, a shrubbery or a stand of woody perennials on terraced steps between the low walls (see p. 37). Fruit trees or vegetables planted in rows across the slope will thrive as long as it is not a north-facing slope.

From sketch to reality

Proceed in the following sequence:
● Write down all of the wishes of your family with respect to the garden and, after careful consideration, make a choice among all these features, trying to cater for everyone if possible.
● Try to retain already existing, established stands of wood.
● Make inquiries well in advance regarding any existing laws or regulations, particularly with respect to minimum distances from boundaries.
● Consult gardening books and nursery catalogues before choosing materials and plants and note the prices.
● Make a sketch of your plot of land, along with an outline of the buildings, windows and doors, on a scale of at least 1:100. This means that 1 m in reality will be represented by 1 cm on your drawing. Draw in neighbouring buildings and trees. Lay a piece of transparent paper over the drawing and sketch in your garden ideas. You can use as many sheets of transparent paper as you wish to make any number of plans.
● If you need help with this, you can always seek out an experienced landscape gardener who will be able to answer all your questions.
● If you intend to create slopes, hollows or similar in a brand-new garden, this is best carried out after the basic structure of the building has gone up.
● The first things to build are a patio, a sitting area, walls and paths, pergolas and support frames and fences.
● Next order the top soil and have it spread around the plot.
● If necessary, improve it with sand or compost.
● Plant the larger trees and bushes first, then fruit trees and herbaceous perennials, with ground-covering plants last.
● In the remaining spaces, establish areas for perennials, summer flowers, vegetables and herbs. Consider the various requirements for light of different plants. If you are doing this work in the spring, you can start planting right away. If the garden is being created in the autumn, it is a good idea to give the soil a boost by planting green fertilizer plants (see table, p. 31).
● Once the beds have been established, you can sow lawns.

Planning and building

Reinforced paths, flat areas and steps

You will need to construct a reinforced area right beside the house where you may need to walk in all kinds of weather.

● Finely structured gravelled areas can be easily and inconspicuously integrated into a small garden. These will have to be supplemented with fresh gravel every few years if they are to continue to look neat and tidy. Do not build paths immediately beside a housewall, but keep them at a distance from the walls (for example, by dividing them off with a strip of coarse gravel). In this way you can always negotiate the path comfortably with bulky loads (watering can, basket, wheelbarrow).

● Small paving stones can be integrated in a particularly harmonious fashion in small gardens.

● Large paving stones or slabs do not look so good in narrow paths. Laid in large areas, they suffocate the garden visually.

● A paving made of concrete will seal the ground against weeds but you must also consider that some types of surface can become very slippery in winter and will not stand strewing with salt.

● Gravel is a very reasonably priced surfacing medium and will often be sufficient for the back garden. It also drains well. It is safe in icy weather but can be difficult to run a wheelbarrow over.

Tips on laying a surface: It is rarely necessary to lay paving stones or slabs on a concrete base. Usually, a bed of sand will be sufficient. The surface should slope away from the house slightly to allow for drainage. The more cracks there are between paving stones and slabs, the more easily drained the reinforced area will become.

Materials for reinforcing an area

Natural paving stones can be obtained in great variety. They look good and are indestructible and timeless.

Frost-proof bricks are obtainable in yellow, brown and red as well as in different sizes.

Concrete stones and slabs are available in many colours and in varying quality. They are cheap and easy to lay.

Concrete grid slabs are used for reinforcing an area and allow grass to grow through the holes.

Wooden paving looks natural but will become slippery in wet weather. Soft wood does not last long; hard wood is relatively expensive.

Gravel for paths and other areas is a cheap and natural solution.

Making small gardens more interesting

Try to integrate your garden with its surroundings. If the immediate environs are particularly attractive (for example, a beautiful landscape, conspicuous features in the terrain, historical building), design your garden boundaries in such a way that there is an unimpeded view. Ugly surroundings, such as high walls, factories or housewalls, may be covered in foliage (after coming to an agreement with the owner) or else planting trees or bushes may obscure them entirely.

The practice of dividing up small, narrow gardens into several different areas has a special charm of its own, particularly if the individual sections afford views into other parts of the garden and therefore give an impression of surprisingly greater width and size. Cleverly conceived and planned gardens only reveal details as you are walking through them. This gives the impression that the actual area of the garden is much greater than it really is. One should be able to glimpse only a small part of the next section of the garden from any point along a path. On the other hand, this should not tempt one to build unnecessarily winding paths which encourage people to take short cuts across flowerbeds (see p. 19).

Help from the experts

Coming up with ideas of your own is still worthwhile even if you do decide to consult a professional garden planner. If you present him or her with your particular wishes, you will be able to have your very own individual and unique garden. You will find the names and telephone numbers of garden architects in your local *Yellow Pages* directory. Some tree nurseries and garden centres also offer garden planning services. Obviously, such work can be expensive and you must make certain to get properly detailed quotations before the work begins. It is also a good idea to visit gardens open to the public and garden exhibitions etc. to seek inspiration. There you will see numerous ideas relating to the construction of paths and walls as well as for working and designing with wood. Garden landscapers and plant nurseries often have information stands at such exhibitions. The garden trade also provides very informative publications and catalogues. Finally, do not forget casual conversations with garden owners of many years' standing. Also, when out for a walk, take a look over garden fences or hedges and study the layout and features.

Paths

A path as a continuation of steps
Steps can lead down into the garden from a patio and then continue as a path. The path is flanked by shrubs or tall perennials. The garden seat will only gradually become visible as you reach the bottom of the steps.

A path as a divider of vegetable and ornamental gardens
Left of the path are the vegetable beds; on the right is a flowerbed with plants of different heights and colours to provide variety. The path will lead right through the splendour of the garden.

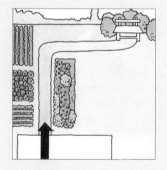

A path as a dividing element
Straight paths are often boring. It is a good idea to connect certain "goals" in the garden by means of a curving path. The bends in the path should be flanked by shrubs to give them a reason for being there. The shrubs also help to divide up the garden harmoniously.

Building paths, walls and steps

The basic rule for paths is that the path to the front door should be about 1.2 m (4 ft) wide; the other paths at least 60 cm (2 ft) wide.

Building paths
(illustration 1)

Method
● Measure the area of the path, leaving an extra 5 cm (2 in) on each side, and mark the edges with pegs and string.
● Dig out the soil to a depth of about 25 cm (10 in). The path should slope slightly to each side by about 3 cm (1¼ in) per metre (40 in) of path so that water can run away easily.
● Place a 20 cm (8 in) thick layer of gravel or coarse grit on the path surface and stamp it down to a thickness of 15 cm (6 in).
● Add a 5 cm (2 in) layer of finer gravel or grit on top, then damp it and stamp it down. Repeat this with a

second layer of fine gravel.
● Add a 3 cm (1¼ in) layer of sand which should then be levelled and rolled.
● Provided the base is sufficiently thick, such gravel or concrete paths will support the weight of cars etc.
● Save some remnants of the covering layer for repairs later on.

Side reinforcement
This is not absolutely essential for paths but will increase their durability. Paving, border or edging stones should be bedded in a foundation of concrete (see illustration 1). These edging stones can also be placed on the lowest gravel layer (see illustration 2). The outermost row ends where the soil begins. Protruding edges are unattractive and will interfere with lawn care.

Paving
(illustrations 2, 3 and 4)

Pavements should be constructed with a 5:100 degree slope to the sides.
● On top of the stamped-down layer of gravel mentioned above, add a 5 cm (2 in) thick layer of sand and smooth it over.
● Concrete paving stones can be evenly laid on top of this layer,

the cracks are filled with sand and the entire surface is knocked down firmly.
● Natural stones will have to be laid individually and tapped down firmly with a paving mallet. Finally, add sand over the paved surface, level it and sweep it into the cracks.

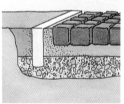

1 A gravel path with concrete reinforcement.

2 A cobbled path with sunken edging stones.

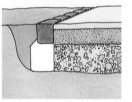

3 Natural stones in rows.

4 A pattern in slabs and smaller stones.

This procedure should be repeated again after a few weeks.

My tip: Worn or secondhand natural paving stones can be used just like new ones and are considerably cheaper.

Drystone walls
(illustration 5)

The best-looking walls are those that have been built using local stone. When building, make sure that all the stones end up lying flat.
● First of all, mark the course of the wall with string.
● Dig out the foundations to about 40 cm (16 in) deep with a slight inclination away from any slope.
● Use coarse gravel as a drainage layer. In the case of steeper slopes, an additional drainage pipe behind the wall will also become necessary.
● Choose stones that are as large as possible for the first layer, to fill up the entire width of the wall.
● If necessary, lay smaller stones underneath irregularly formed large stones.

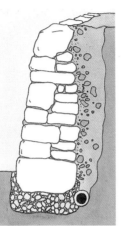

5 A drystone wall made of natural stones.

● Cracks between stones should be bridged by stones lying above them.
● Never lay more than two courses of narrow stones beside a thicker stone.
● While building the wall, you can plant trailing perennials in the cracks together with a little soil.
● While building, note that the wall should lean slightly away from the direction of a slope (10-20:100 incline).
● Keep filling up the gap behind the wall with rubble and larger stones while building, and with packed-in soil between the stones and the slope.
● The top layer should consist of larger stones to make it more stable.

Steps
(illustrations 6 and 7)

All steps should be designed to accommodate the average length of a footstep, according to the formula: 2 x height + surface of step = 64; 70 for shallower steps. If the step is 15 cm (6 in) high, for example, the step itself should be 34 cm (13½ in) wide; if the height is 12 cm (4¾ in), the surface will be 46 cm (about 18½ in). Stable steps can be built out of slabs set on edge in most ground covering materials (see illustration 6). Wooden batten steps held in position by posts (see illustration 7) are cheaper but will not last as long.

Side reinforcements consisting of edging slabs or natural stone will emphasize the course of the steps but can often look alien in a garden. Instead, plant ground-covering plants or herbaceous perennials along the edges to form a harmonious transition from steps to garden.

6 Cobbled steps are particularly durable.

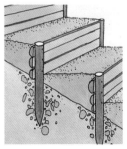

7 Wooden steps made of planks.

A garden all in green, but not at all boring.
On the left is a pond for goldfish.
Climbing roses, clematis, ivy and vines disguise the walls. The sitting area is raised.

Building sitting areas

A patio is not the only place where one can sit out as even the front garden or somewhere behind the house may yield a corner for a garden seat. During the seasons you can utilize the sunniest spot in spring or autumn; in the height of the summer you might prefer a shadier nook. Sitting areas situated on the east, south or west sides of the house, together with shade-giving woody plants and pergolas, will provide their own daily and annual schedule of sunlight. A leafy roof provided by trees will integrate the sitting area with the rest of the garden.

A sunken sitting area: A particularly restful atmosphere is created by sitting areas that are situated 20-50 cm (8-20 in) lower than the surrounding area. Usually, a lot of soil will have to be dug out for this purpose and the extra effort does, at first, seem rather daunting. The best time to plan such a feature is while a house is being built. It is important to create drainage or some form of run-off to carry water away from the spot. You will be amazed, however, at how much larger your garden will look from this position! The edges of the sunken area can be bordered by a grass verge, a drystone wall or a wall low enough to sit on. The latter should be equipped with cover slabs that are comfortable for sitting on.

Size of the sitting area: The sitting area should be big enough to accommodate all family members and perhaps a few large containers of plants. It is not a good idea to make the sitting area very large just so that you can have a garden party once a year and accommodate all your friends. Such a party can take place all over the garden. Remember, when planning, that a small table with two chairs requires an area of 4 sq m (about 4 sq yd), with six chairs 12 sq m (12 sq yd), and a garden seat with an approach to it 3 sq m (3 sq yd).

Pergolas and fences

Pergolas offer shade and divide up the garden. They also provide a visual screen and shelter from wind. A pergola that is situated right beside a building looks particularly pleasing and forms a pleasant transition to the garden. Pergolas tend to look a little lost if they are not positioned close to a wall or tree.

Typical pergolas consist of vertical support posts and horizontal weight-bearing elements that support cross pieces. The closer together the latter are installed, the more shade is given by the structure. Pergolas come in various sizes. Rounded posts look rustic, square posts more utilitarian. The thickness of the posts should be in keeping with the total size of the structure and the same goes for the distance between the cross pieces which, as a rule, varies between 50-80 cm (20-32 in).

Additional trellises and climbing plants between the support posts will ensure a sheltered position. They provide a visual screen, protection from wind and may be used as space dividers or fences. Wood is the most often used material for this purpose and it looks most attractive if it is left natural. Garden owners will be doing themselves a favour if they buy ready made, pressure-treated timber. Just consider the necessity of having to repaint every few years if you decide to paint the wood!

Fences are intended to create boundaries but should not appear unwelcoming. The type of fence to choose will often be stipulated on the building plans. Wooden fences look good in nearly all gardens. Thick walls and massive fence posts take up too much room and look heavy and forbidding in small gardens. All boundaries look better with some greenery, for example, nasturtiums, roses or other climbing plants. A bedful of flowers and plants looks particularly inviting and generous in front of a fence.

Espaliers, palisades and fences

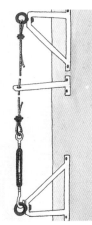

Removable espaliers and climbing wires that can be clipped off make it easier to get at a wall if the façade needs repair work etc.

Wires and espaliers
(illustrations 1 and 2)

A distance from the wall of about 20 cm (8 in) is important for both fixtures so that air can circulate sufficiently. Specialist shops offer a wide range of kits to suit every taste. Choose a stable construction which will cope with the weight of plants and pressure from the wind. Plastic-coated wires and attachments made of galvanized metal are very durable. Insert spacers between long wires (see illustration 1). **My tip:** Different plants require different climbing aids (see p. 45).
● The individual struts should not be too thick

for climbing plants to cling to.
● Winding plants can manage to spiral around thicker battens.
● Woody species should be trained up wooden supports. Thin wires may constrict the shoots later on. Now and again, tie individual branches or shoots to their support. Make the ties in the shape of a figure of eight loop around the shoot and the support. Make absolutely sure that the plant will not be constricted.

1 Wires drawn taut are ideal for climbing plants.

● Some climbing plants do not require any climbing aid. Ivy (*Hedera* species), climbing hydrangeas (*Hydrangea anomala petiolaris*) and Virginia creeper (*Parthenocissus tricuspidata*) are experts

at clinging to walls. **NB:** Never grow these plants on damaged rendering! They may grow into the cracks and damage the stonework further.

Palisades
(illustration 3)

Differences in heights may be softened with palisades which will also provide protection from the wind.

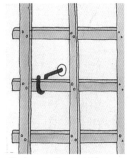

2 A wooden grid hung on angle irons.

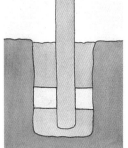

3 Tall palisades should be concreted in.

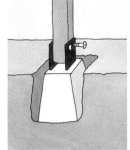

4 Do not set posts straight into the soil.

Low palisades can be anchored in a gravel bed; taller ones will need the additional support provided by being set in a layer of concrete. Along a slope, a layer of roofing felt between the wood and the soil will ensure a longer life for the wood.

Support posts
(illustration 4)

Never insert wooden supports straight into the soil as they would quickly rot. Screw them into a stable post shoe that should stand in a concrete foundation. Various models for anchoring support posts can be obtained in the trade.

Wood protection

Really effective wood protection agents cannot avoid being toxic. Treated wood should not be burnt but needs to be disposed off as sensitive waste. Please note the following points regarding wood protection agents.
● Only wooden structures that have to last a very long time should be treated with chemical agents.
● Wood-preserving agents containing creosote will release harmful substances to plants, particularly in sunny weather.
● Wood that has been pressure treated using boron and copper salts is recommended. Buy wood in which the protective agent has penetrated to a minimum depth of over 1 cm (just less than ½ in). Note that the colour on the outside gives no indication as to the quality of impregnation.
● Any places where the wood has holes bored into it or is sawn after treatment will require more treatment with boron salts. Painting it by hand, even with several coats, will never attain a sufficient depth.
● Use durable woods like robinia, oak, larch and pine.
● Make sure the wood is seasoned and has been stored properly.
● Avoid the direct contact of the wood with the soil by building foundations of gravel or

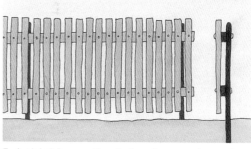

5 A picket fence will suit almost any garden and any surroundings.

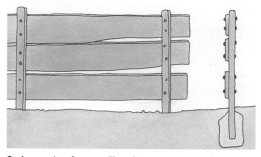

6 A wooden fence will make a narrow garden appear wider and is strong and weather resistant.

ready-mixed concrete.
● Make sure that water can easily run off all parts of the wood, both from the structure itself and into the soil.

Fences
(illustrations 4, 5 and 6)

Many types of fencing can be bought in prefabricated sections.

Pressure-treated posts may be driven straight into the soil (see illustration 5), may be concreted in (illustration 6) or fixed in a concrete socket (illustration 4).

Planning and building

Lighting in your garden

Lighting will be necessary in the front garden for safety and security reasons alone. In a back garden, it can lend a certain charm to a warm summer's night. Lights that switch themselves on and off when someone moves through a field around them are both practical and save money. New models are now on the market that do not even require connecting to mains electricity as they are powered by solar energy. They are ideal for any remoter corner of the garden. Do not choose lamps that are too conspicuous. Round or cylindrical shapes go with curved paths; angular ones look better in gardens that have plenty of right-angled features.

The right position: Give some thought to where you will put the lamps. All important paths should be lit so that you can walk along them at night without tripping up. Lamps are necessary at an entrance door, on patios, sitting areas, bends in paths and on steps. In addition to this, you may also wish to illuminate sculptures, interesting plants, the pond, a bird bath and attractive bushes or trees.

Garden taps

Most areas of the garden, in particular ornamental lawns, vegetable gardens and splendid flowerbeds, will require watering during the summer months. In the case of detached houses, it is a good idea to install taps on opposite sides of the house. A further tap for an outside shower in the garden will ensure a welcome and refreshing experience for both adults and children on hot summer days. A water basin to catch water has the advantage that rainwater can warm up in it. This is particularly good for watering plants.

Any form of rainwater collector is very useful. In the case of a newly built house, it may even be possible to plan in an underground cistern. The size will depend on the area of garden (about 1.5-3 cu m/cu yd for a garden of 300 sq m/sq yd) and will also depend on whether you want to use soft rainwater for your WC or washing machine in the house.

Compost

Recycling garden and kitchen refuse in your own garden is an important contribution towards looking after the environment and helps with the ever-increasing cost of refuse and waste disposal. Even the smallest of gardens will produce staggering amounts of green stuff for composting. Compost is able to turn mediocre soils into humus-rich garden soil in a matter of a few years.

Composter for small gardens: The decision to start composting in a small garden is not always an easy one to make. Nevertheless, you need not have a large, ugly compost heap. For a small composting station, one to three composters made of recycled plastic, wooden battens, round posts or dense wire netting may be sufficient.

Where to site the composting station: Generally, a composting station should be situated right on the edge of the garden, mainly for aesthetic reasons. It should also be positioned in such a way that it will offend neither you nor your neighbours. The important thing with open composting stations is that they are in a slightly shady and sheltered position so that they do not dry out or cool down too quickly.

Lights near water will create reflections and prevent accidents. More lights are situated along the stream.

Designing a composting station: They can be hidden behind dense woody shrubs like forsythia or hydrangea or surrounded by tall flowering plants like yarrow, sunflowers, campion or golden rod. Fruit bushes will also provide a visual screen. A shade-providing tree is also a good solution; for example, an apple tree. Open compost heaps can be surrounded by gourds or nasturtium which will spread over the heap. Study a little composting theory and you will be able to make sure that unpleasant smells can be avoided.

Indirect light from the house.

A living garden

Planting and sowing

Once the building or alteration procedures are finished you can start planting trees and shrubs and sow a lawn. There is a whole range of possibilities for different designs. If the soil is poor, however, the first thing to do is to undertake a course of soil improvement.

Left: A small, formally designed ornamental garden with perennials and spherical box trees. The large container can be planted with a variety of seasonal flowers.
Above: Phacelia tanacetifolia produces flowers in an enchanting shade of blue and makes an excellent green fertilizer plant.

Planting and sowing

The planting plan

First of all, you must create a planting plan on which you mark in the locations of trees and shrubs. While doing this, remember that trees often grow very fast so you should make sure that you place them far enough apart. You will find the recommended spacing for plants on their labels or in a good catalogue.

Shrubberies are usually planted more densely than recommended so that they look good during the first year. After a year or two, however, you will have to move plants that are growing too closely together. These small corrections are part of the routine annual jobs in a garden.

Soil preparation

The soil is usually particularly damaged during the building of a house. Before the building begins, during dry weather, the topsoil and lower layer should be removed and stored in separate heaps. These heaps should be protected by sowing a crop of green fertilizer on them. When the house construction is over, the compacted soil all around the building should be mechanically broken up. Then, again in dry weather, replace the lower layer of soil and let it settle for a while before covering it with the topsoil. Already established areas of the garden with compacted soil can be loosened up with a rotivator. Builders or agricultural machine suppliers will do this for you.

Simple digging over of the topsoil surface will be sufficient preparation for sowing a lawn, a vegetable patch and summer flowerbeds. The best time for this is late autumn before the ground becomes frozen.

Tips for different soils
● Wet soils are easy to dig over if they have frozen superficially on the surface. Once this is done, this area only needs raking over before sowing or planting in the spring.
● Very heavy soils should only be worked over by machine under exceptional circumstances. They will look looser following this treatment but will become even harder and more solid afterwards.
● The use of a rotary hoe is ideal in sandy, slightly loamy soils.

Buying topsoil: Very often, your own topsoil will have become contaminated with building rubble and you will need to buy extra topsoil. Buying loose, sieved topsoil, which is a little more expensive, will pay for itself in the long run. Make sure it is good quality when delivered.
● A rich brown colour indicates a high humus content.
● The soil should be slightly sandy and loamy.
● Objects like large stones or plastic debris should not be present.
● The soil should not contain the roots of tough and durable weeds like couch grass or convolvulus.

My tip: While the house is being built, try to ensure that no lime-rich building rubble or even debris from rendering or painting is deposited in the garden.

Improving the soil

Humus-rich soil with a medium content of sand and clay offers the best conditions of nutrients and water retention for soil organisms and plant roots. Topsoil which does not conform to these requirements should be improved.

Soils poor in humus
● Mix in bark humus, compost, peat or animal manure; about 600 litres (130 gal) per 100 sq m/sq yd.

Green fertilizer plants for small gardens

Plant	Soil	Earliest sowing	Latest sowing	Development time in weeks	Remarks
Calendula officinalis marigold	all soils	esp	ms	12	Wards off nematodes. Flowers yellow and orange.
Lupinus albus white lupin	heavy	esp	ls	12	Fixes nitrogen. Flowers white.
Phacelia tanacetifolia	all soils	esp	ea	8	Attracts bees. Flowers blue.
Sinapis alba white mustard	medium	esp	ea	6-8	Do not plant before brassicas. Flowers yellow.
Tagetes patula	all soils	esp	lsp	8-10	Wards off nematodes. Flowers yellow, orange, brown.
Trifolium incarnatum long-headed clover	medium to heavy	esp	ls	12	Fixes nitrogen. Flowers red.
Tropaeolum majus nasturtium	medium	lsp	ls	6-8	Flowers all summer; yellow, orange, red.

Key: esp = early spring; msp = mid spring; lsp = late spring; s = summer; a = autumn; w = winter

● If necessary, plant green fertilizer several times.
● Plant potatoes in the first year, as they loosen the soil.

Clay-rich soils
● Work in a 5 cm (2 in) thick layer of sand.
● Sow one lot of green fertilizer and dig over roughly in the autumn.

Sandy soils
● Spread compost and sow green fertilizer.
● Work in clay-rich soil.

Green fertilizer

Sowing a crop of green fertilizer before planting will greatly improve the soil if it is poor in humus, very heavy or very sandy. These plants enrich the soil with humus and prevent an area that is not planted immediately from becoming infested with weeds. Fast-growing, deep-rooting plants will penetrate the subsoil and ensure a permanent loosening effect. Most green fertilizer plants can be sown from spring until the end of the second month of summer. After that, plant only the particularly fast-growing types which have their main growth period up until the second month of autumn (see table above). Several crops in succession are also advantageous. Fully grown plants should be cut down and then worked into the soil in a shallow manner after a few days. Should you require the area for sowing immediately, compost the green fertilizer plants separately.

Planting and sowing

A little apple tree will fit in even the smallest garden. Espalier fruit trees can be grown along a housewall, as a hedge along a fence or as a dividing element in a garden. This small apple tree (variety "Elstar") trained in the shape of a double U shows just how attractive espalier fruit trees can be.

Woody plants for small gardens

Always observe the rules of minimum spacing (see p. 13) when planting and make sure you know the sizes when fully mature of the trees and bushes you are planting. Trees with small crowns require a distance of 3-4 m (10-13 ft) from your house or a neighbouring property. Provided you come to an agreement with your neighbours, you could also plant a tree directly on the boundary to save space. If you do not want a tree near your house, plant a tall shrub instead. By using shrubs, you can also:
● create a colourful shrubbery
● set a boundary along the outside of your property, maybe even replacing a fence
● divide the garden up into separate areas.
Indigenous trees and shrubs provide food and shelter for numerous insect and bird species. Many such bushes, however, will grow too vigorously for a small garden so it becomes almost essential to employ adaptable foreign species. You can obtain help and advice from a good nursery or from a good plant catalogue. Varieties with very colourful foliage should be used with discretion as they can look too conspicuous in a group.

Planting trees

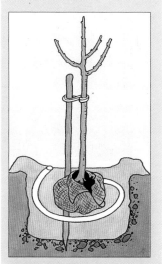

● Dig a large planting hole.
● Separate the topsoil from the subsoil.
● Loosen the floor of the hole with a garden fork.
● Drive in a support post.
● Lay a drainage pipe if the soil is very heavy or will be paved over later on. The pipe should emerge above the surface.
● Stand the tree in the hole at the same depth as it was planted before. For fruit trees, the grafting point should be 15 cm (6 in) above the ground.
● Open out the wrapping (if any) around the rootstock.
● Replace subsoil, then topsoil and tread it down.
● Tie the tree to its post and water well (40 litres/9 gal water).

Conifers

These prickly, evergreen trees are not very suitable for providing shade in small gardens. How would you like to lie down under a spruce tree in your bathing suit? Deciduous trees, on the other hand, create dappled shade and allow sunlight to penetrate during the winter. Anyway, many moisture-loving conifers only feel really at home in mountainous regions. Conifer hedges will require a severe pruning after several years, which will leave ugly scars. Deciduous trees, on the other hand, can be rejuvenated again and again by cutting back.
Individual indigenous evergreens can still liven up a stand of trees and shrubs: the yew (*Taxus baccata*) will prove a valuable shade giver, although it is very toxic and perhaps it should be avoided if you have young children and domestic pets. Common juniper (*Juniperus communis*) and pine (*Pinus mugo*) make good evergreen companions for shrubs but you should definitely avoid a collection of dwarf varieties! They do not make effective dividing elements in a garden.

Planting and sowing

Correct planting

Name	Position Height in m	Flowering time Colour	Ornamental fruit (x) Edible fruit (e)	Remarks
Amelanchier laevis snowy mespilus	○ – ◐ 5	msp white	e	Large bush, attractive autumn foliage; for a flowering hedge.
Berberis thunbergii barberry	◐ – ● 0.5-2	msp yellow	x	For a flowering and trimmed hedge.
Buddleia alternifolia buddleia	○ 4	es violet	–	For a flowering hedge, hanging over a wall.
Buddleia davidii	○ 2-3	ms white, violet	–	For a shrubbery and freestanding.
Buxus sempervirens var *arborescens*	○ – ● 4	green	–	Evergreen; for trimmed and freely growing hedge.
Buxus sempervirens "Suffruticosa"	○ – ● 0.5	green	–	Evergreen; for low growing hedges.
Caryopteris x clandonensis	○ – ◐ 1	ls-ma dark blue	–	For shrubberies and flowering hedges.
Chaenomeles japonica Japanese quince	○ – ◐ 1-2	esp brick red	x	For flowering and untrimmed hedges.
Cornus mas cornelian cherry	○ – ● 6	lw yellow	e	For flowering and trimmed hedges; as large tree beside house.
Corylopsis pauciflora	◐ 1.5	esp yellow	–	For flowering hedge and freestanding.
Cotoneaster dammeri cotoneaster	○ – ◐ 0.5	lsp-es white	x	As a groundcovering plant; hanging over walls.
Crataegus species ornamental thorn	○ 6	lsp white, pink	x	As a trimmed hedge; large tree beside a house.
Cytisus species broom	○ 0.5-2	msp yellow, pink	x	For a flowering hedge.
Daphne mezereum ☠	○ – ● –	esp violet	x	For a flowering hedge; with trees.
Deutzia gracilis	○ 0.8	lsp white	–	For a flowering hedge.
Erica carnea heather	○ 0.3	ew-esp white, purple	–	As a groundcover plant.
Hamamelis x intermedia witch hazel	○ 2-4	esp yellow, red	–	Freestanding.
Hamamelis virginiana	○ 3-5	la-ew light yellow	–	Freestanding.
Hedera helix ivy ☠	◐ – ● –	ea yellow green	x	As a groundcover plant; climber.
Hippophae rhamnoides	○ 4	msp green	e	As an untrimmed hedge.
Hypericum species St John's wort	○ – ◐ 0.3-0.5	ms yellow	–	As a groundcover plant.
Ilex aquifolium "Alaska" holly	◐ – ● 3	lsp white	x	Evergreen; for hedges.
Jasminum nudiflorum winter jasmine	○ – ◐ 2	lw-esp yellow	–	As an espalier; along walls.

34

Trees and shrubs for small gardens

Name		Position Height in m	Flowering time Colour	Ornamental fruit (x) Edible fruit (e)	Remarks
Kerria japonica		◐ 2	lsp yellow	–	For flowering hedges and freestanding.
Kolkwitzia amabilis beauty bush		◐ 2	lsp pink	–	For flowering hedges.
Laburnum x watereri laburnum	☠	○ 4	lsp yellow	x	For a flowering hedge; as a tree beside the house.
Ligustrum vulgare	☠	○ — ◐ 3-5	es-ms white	x	For flowering and cut hedges.
Ligustrum vulgare "Lodense"	☠	○ — ◐ 0.5-1	es-ms white	x	For a low, trimmed hedge.
Ligustrum vulgare "Atrovirens"	☠	○ — ◐ 5	es-ms white	x	For a taller, trimmed hedge.
Lonicera pileata honeysuckle	☠	○ — ● 1	lsp yellow white	x	As groundcover.
Lonicera xylosteum fly honeysuckle	☠	○ — ● 1-3	lsp white, yellow	x	For a flowering and trimmed hedge.
Mahonia aquifolium Oregon grape		○ — ● 1	msp yellow	x	Evergreen; for shrubbery and freestanding.
Pachysandra terminalis		● 0.4	msp-lsp white	–	As groundcover.
Philadelphus species mock orange		○ 1-4	es white	–	For a flowering or untrimmed hedge.
Potentilla fruticosa		○ 0.2-1	lsp-ms yellow, pink	–	For a low hedge; as groundcover.
Prunus subhirtella cherry		○ — ◐ 4	msp white pink	–	For a flowering hedge and freestanding.
Prunus species		○ 6	msp white	x	As a tree beside a house.
Pyracantha coccinea firethorn		○ — ◐ 3	lsp white	x	As a flowering hedge.
Ribes alpinum "Schmidt" flowering currant		◐ — ◑ 1.5	msp yellow	–	For a cut hedge.
Sorbus aria common whitebeam		○ — ◐ 8-10	lsp white	x	As a tree beside a house.
Spiraea japonica		○ — ◐ 0.5	es-ms pink	–	As groundcover and for hedges.
Syringa microphylla lilac		○ — ◐ 1.5	lsp white, red, lilac	–	For a flowering hedge.
Syringa reflexa		○ 3	es-ms pink	–	For a flowering hedge.
Taxus baccata yew	☠	○ — ● 10	ms green	x	Evergreen; for a trimmed hedge and as a tree beside the house.
Viburnum species	☠	○ — ● 1-3	lsp-es white	x	For a flowering hedge.
Vinca minor lesser periwinkle		◐ — ● 0.4	msp-lsp blue	–	As groundcover.
Weigela species		◐ — ● 1-3	es red	–	As a flowering hedge.

Key: esp = early spring; msp = mid spring; lsp = late spring; s = summer; a = autumn; w = winter

Planting and sowing

Planting bulbs and perennials

In the winter, these plants die back into their rootstocks or bulbs. Once they are planted, they will survive for years in your garden. Some species belong to the early-flowering types, others produce shoots very cautiously to begin with but will go on flowering until the first frosts. The charm of perennials lies in watching one type of plant after another flowering in succession in the same bed. This means that, even in a small garden, you can have different flowers and colours all year round in the same spot. The best way to proceed is to plant bedding plants in groups, combined with trees and shrubs and bush roses. Planting time is in the autumn or spring or during the rest phase of the respective species.

Tall perennials are planted in groups of at least two or three, smaller ones in groups of five to fifteen. Spacing of the plants will depend on their speed of growth. You will usually find such information on the plant labels or in a good book on herbaceous perennials. Perennials can be divided into two large groups:

Cultivated hybrids and varieties: These include large-flowered cultivars like peony (*Paeonia-lactiflora* hybrids) or delphiniums *(Delphinium* hybrids). They will require good soil and also the occasional fertilizing.

Wild flowers: They usually have delicate small flowers in inconspicuous colours and have mostly retained their original characters. They will require hardly any care in a suitable position.

The age of perennials: Some long-lived plants, like *Helleborus niger*, peony (*Paeonia-lactiflora* hybrids), day lilies (*Hemerocallis* hybrids) and bleeding heart (*Dicentra spectabilis*) will develop best if they are allowed to grow undisturbed.

In the case of most perennials, like *Phlox paniculata*, the vigour of growth will lessen after four to seven years. At this point the rootstocks should be taken out and divided during their rest phase. Only the most healthy, vigorous parts should then be replanted in soil improved with compost.

There are also some particularly short-lived perennials that should be planted again about every two years: asters (*Aster alpinus*), *Coreopsis grandiflora* and shasta daisies (*Chrysanthemum maximum*).

Sowing a lawn

The best time for seeding is during the last days of spring or in early autumn. The soil should be loosened up beforehand and improved (see p. 30) as this will make the lawn much easier to care for later on. Find the right seed mixture: for example, for an ornamental lawn or play area and for a sunny or shady position. Sow half of the seed by hand and then repeat this exercise as this will ensure a more even distribution. Finally, rake the seed in shallowly and press down. The seed should not be allowed to dry out before the lawn has become properly established. If you neglect this aspect the result will be a patchy lawn!

A "gravel" lawn: This area can be driven over and will still provide a green area. Spread a thin layer of topsoil on a gravel layer. A special seed mixture will be required for sowing. The seed should be evenly distributed and raked in. Most of the soil should disappear into the gravel layer. Grid stones with grass growing through them make even better weight-bearers than gravel lawns. The grid stones are laid on top of a reinforced foundation (see pp. 20/21), then topsoil is spread on top and seed is sown as for a "gravel" lawn.

Gardening on a slope

The advice of an expert can prove invaluable when designing a garden on a slope. All too often, a concrete wall is built in a hurry and can then only be disguised with difficulty later on. A natural stone wall has a much more attractive effect and can be built to a height of 1.5 m (5 ft) even as a drystone wall without mortar (see pp. 20/21). Should you wish to plant trees or shrubs, perennials, annuals or vegetables on a slope, this is just as easy to do on several terraces and small slopes that have been built with the support of several low walls. A planting of shrubs and trees amid stones on a slope that has been constructed to look natural will look particularly pretty. When using random rocks or stones for integration in a verge or sloping bed, you should always lay them on their broadest side. Stones standing on edge tend to fall over easily and may squash plants or roll down the slope. They will also create shadow on the soil whereas flatter stones conduct the sun's warmth through the soil to plant roots and thus create a typical rockery climate.

Beds on slopes

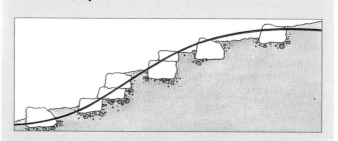

The incline of a slope can be softened with stones and low walls. **NB:** Sink the stones into the soil along their longest edges so that some can function as stepping stones. This will create an attractive rockery.

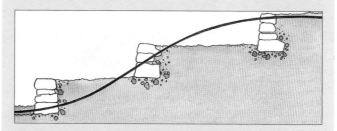

A slope can also be divided up into individual terraces with several low walls. In this way, you can create beds for small shrubs, roses, perennials or vegetables.

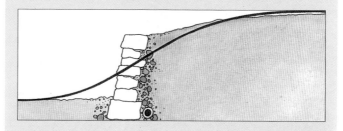

If you wish, you can support a steep slope with a drystone wall. Cut a "step" into the slope and build the drystone wall so that two levels are created.

Tips on designing

Cosy nooks for adults to relax in, play areas for children and splendid beds need to be planned and designed properly. In the following pages you will find many ideas for designing your garden.

Left: A garden planted only with trees and shrubs can look most attractive. Varieties with coloured foliage add something to the arrangement. A further advantage is that gardens like this are easy to look after.
Above: Enchanting colours can be achieved just from the foliage of different shrubs.

Tips on designing

A sitting area beside a pergola covered in roses and clematis.

A combined patio, sitting area and pond.

Planting around a patio

If the sitting area is near the house, you will be able to design three sides according to your own personal preferences. A visual screen is rarely necessary on all sides. Plant a varied collection of plants of different heights around the patio. The following are particularly attractive examples.

A sitting area among roses:
● Climbing and bush roses make a good visual screen.
● You may wish to plant blue companion plants like lavender (*Lavandula officinalis*) or summer sage (*Salvia nemorosa*) between bedding roses.
● Ground-cover roses are ideal for verges, slopes and walls.

Mediterranean sitting area:
How about a grapevine espalier as a visual screen with ripe grapes ready to pick in the autumn? A corner like this can be framed with scented plants. Colourful large container plants will round off the picture.

A sunny rockery: A drystone wall frames a sunken sitting area well. Recumbent stones, low-growing perennials and cushions harmonize well with such an arrangement. A flowering hedge or taller plants will provide a visual screen at the side.

A woodland sitting area: Taller growing bushes will provide a woodland glade atmosphere in shady positions that can be planted with shade-loving perennials and ferns according to your wishes.

A cosy garden nook in the shade.

Somewhere to sit

The more places there are in which to sit and dream, the more comfortable and enjoyable your garden will become. For this reason, many garden owners like to provide more than one sitting area. This may be a garden seat or even a small bower, a drystone wall or a hammock slung between two fruit trees. Several waterproof, folding garden chairs will make the whole arrangement very flexible.

A place for children

A simple utilitarian lawn will make an ideal play area.

Sand box or tray: A stable sand box, if possible in semi-shade, is a must for small children. It should be equipped with a cover as protection against dogs, cats and falling leaves.

Playthings: Swings, slides, bouncy figures, climbing frames and a netball basket will complete a children's play area. Choose one or two stable models that may be anchored on a piece of lawn or in sand for safety reasons. The spacing between pieces of play equipment should be wide enough so that a child falling from one of them is not able to injure itself or another child. Any concrete plinths should end a few centimetres under the surface of the soil.

Playhouses and tents: Children love to retreat inside their own four walls. You can provide a readymade playhouse, a Wendy house, a homemade hut made of planks or a tent made of canvas or beanpoles that can be planted with annual climbing plants during the summer (see p. 45). An older fruit tree may support a tree house or at least a solid, reinforced sitting plank. These structures should not be situated too high for reasons of safety.

A small wild area, garden pond, drystone wall and nesting facilities will provide a large number of creatures with living accommodation and older children, in particular, can be encouraged to observe this wildlife. It must be made absolutely clear to the children that wild creatures are not to be teased or handled.

A child's garden: Many children enjoy having their own little patch where they can plant and sow to their hearts' content.

Designing with trees and shrubs

Trees and shrubs give visual depth to a garden.
● They may divide it horizontally into several areas.
● They even make it possible to design vertically as they will provide the garden with several different levels.

Espalier fruit
(illustration 1)

Visual screens, division into separate areas inside the garden and your own harvest of fruit are all advantages provided by fruit trees grown on espaliers.
Apples and pears: Varieties that are grown as espalier fruit on slow-growing stocks are most suitable. The espalier consists of two, firmly secured, 1.8 m (6 ft) tall posts between which three or four wires are strung at intervals of about 40-60 cm (16-24 in).
The space required by a tree will depend on the variety and stock and an expert will give you advice on this. Espalier trees require regular pruning and you should purchase a specialist book on the subject.
Raspberries and blackberries: These form long shoots that can be tied up and trained along espaliers as visual screens.
My tip: Raspberry varieties that yield two harvests per year are recommended for small gardens. They bear the first fruit in the autumn and a second crop the following summer.

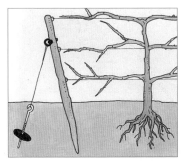

1 Espalier fruit is very suitable for dividing up the garden but requires firm support. The posts must be firmly anchored in the ground.

Trees and shrubs as walls
(illustration 2)

Individual trees or bushes may be used to bring variety into monotonous hedges, to provide a boundary to the garden and will also create interesting features within the garden. A rose arch, for example, is a very decorative way of framing a view but beech trees may also be used when designing paths (see p. 7). You may even cut "windows" into beech hedges. Free-growing hedges look particularly natural, even more so if they are underplanted with perennials. For even the smallest garden, a variety of flowering trees and shrubs can be acquired that need a depth of only about 50 cm (20 in).

2 Trees and bushes as spatial dividers.

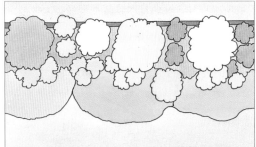

3 A flowering hedge makes an attractive visual screen with perennials planted in front.

A free-standing, 2.5 m (8 ft) wide flowering hedge can be planned as a visual screen along the narrow end of a long, narrow garden.

Designing flowering hedges
(illustration 3)

Make sure you consult plant catalogues in enough time to make the right choices.

● When planting, note the prescribed distances from boundaries.

● For a flowering hedge, choose trees and shrubs that attain different heights and shapes of growth.

● Work out the different flowering times and colours!

● Plant the bushes with sufficient space between them. Many ornamental shrubs, like forsythia (*Forsythia* x *intermedia*), will grow to a width of 3-5 m (10-17 ft) in a few years. The best plan is to leave about 2 m (7 ft) all round for *Forsythia,* instead of spending time and effort later in cutting it back to keep it small. Then it will keep

its shape and look attractive.

● Plant perennials in the gaps between the shrubs. During the first few years you can also sow annual summer flowers but they should not be planted too close to the shrubs.

A trimmed hedge as a garden boundary
(illlustration 4)

If visual screens and shelter from wind are necessary on all sides, you can plant a trimmed hedge consisting of species like common hornbeam (*Carpinus betulus*). This hedge will have to be cut back once a year. Make sure you keep to the minumum prescribed distance from your neighbours' boundaries (see p. 13). This type of hedge will, however, limit your view and will tend to make the garden look smaller.

4 A trimmed hedge will act as a screen but will need clipping once a year.

5 An open boundary makes the garden appear larger by allowing a view to the horizon.

Open garden boundaries
(illustration 5)

Your garden will appear larger if you leave as many open views as possible through to the landscape beyond. This has the effect of making the area beyond it look like part of the garden. Trees make a bold statement and give

structure to the garden. They do not take up much room initially and can spread out over paths. They still allow views beyond the garden, integrate the garden visually with its surroundings and provide welcome shade.

Tips on designing

Climbing plants

Woody climbers

☠ **Clematis** species and hybrids, summer-green plants that use their leaf stalks as tendrils. Height: 3-10 m (10-33 ft). **Warning:** All species are slightly toxic! Recommended varieties:
- "Jackmanii", bluish-violet flowers in mid to late summer.
- "Perle d'Azur", light blue flowers in mid summer to early autumn.
- "Marie Boisselot", pure white, large flowers in early summer to early autumn.
- "Niobe", dark red flowers in early summer to early autumn.
- "The President", purple blue, large flowers in early summer to early autumn.
- "Rouge Cardinal", crimson flowers in early summer to early autumn.
- Clematis viticella "Etoile Violette", dark violet flowers from mid summer to early autumn.
- Clematis tangutica, yellow flowers in early summer to mid autumn.

Dutchman's pipe (Aristolochia macrophylla), summer-green winding plant. Height: to 10 m (33 ft). Greenish-yellow flowers curved like tobacco pipes (insect traps), late spring to early summer.

☠ **Honeysuckle** (Lonicera species), generally a summer-green winding plant. Height: 3-5 m (10-17 ft), white, yellow or reddish scented flowers in early spring to early autumn. **Warning:** The red berries are toxic!

Climbing hydrangea (Hydrangea anomala petiolaris), summer-green climber, up to 5 m (17 ft) tall. White inflorescences in early spring to mid summer.

☠ **Ivy** (Hedera helix), evergreen climber with root suckers, up to 20 m (67 ft) tall. **Warning:** The black berries are extremely toxic!

Kiwi fruit (Actinidia chinensis), summer-green winding plant, dioecious. Height:

4-8 m (13-27 ft). Hardy only in mild regions. Yellow flowers from mid spring, fruit from mid autumn.

Climbing roses (Rosa species), summer-green rambler. Height: 2-5 m (7-17 ft). Flowers of single-flowering types from late spring to early summer; of continuously flowering types early summer to mid autumn.
Recommended varieties:
- "Sympathie", blood-red, scented flowers.
- "New Dawn", whitish-pink, scented flowers.
- "Golden Olympus", golden yellow, scented flowers.
- "Compassion", salmon pink, scented flowers.
- "Super Excelsa", carmine red flowers, small and abundantly flowering.
- "Rosarium Uetersen", deep pink, scented flowers.
- "Direktor Benschop", creamy white flowers, very abundantly flowering but only once annually.

☠ **Russian vine** (Polygonum aubertii), summer-green winding plant. Height: to 15 m (50 ft), white, scented flower spikes in mid summer to mid autumn. **NB:** Grows too fast and abundantly for very small gardens.

Virginia creeper
- Parthenocissus quinquefolia, five-lobed leaves, with winding shoots. Height: to 10 m (33 ft).
- Parthenocissus tricuspidata, tripartite leaves, sucker pads. Height: to 12 m (40 ft). Splendid, longlasting, coloured autumn foliage.

☠ **Wisteria** (Wisteria sinensis), summer-green winding plant, dioecious. Height: to 10 m (33 ft), bluish-violet flowers in mid to late spring. The petals fade and drop naturally. **Warning:** All parts of this plant are toxic!

Annual climbing plants

Black-eyed Susan (Thunbergia alata), winding plant. Height: to 2 m (7 ft). Orange flowers with black centres in early summer to mid autumn. Sheltered position!

Calystegia sepium, winder. Height: to 3 m (10 ft). White to pink flowers in late spring to early autumn.

Cobaea scandens, winding plant. Height: to 4 m (13 ft). Violet, bell-shaped flowers in late summer to mid autumn.

Ornamental gourd (Cucurbita pepo var. ovifera), fast-growing winding plant. Height: to 8 m (27 ft). Yellow flowers, mid summer to mid autumn, conspicuous fruits.

☠ **Morning glory** (Ipomoea tricolor), fast-growing winder. Height: to 5 m (17 ft). Sky blue flowers in mid summer to early autumn. **Warning:** All parts are toxic!

Nasturtium (Tropaeolum majus), uses leaf stalks for climbing. Height: to 2 m (7 ft). Flowers yellow, orange and carmine red in early summer to mid autumn.

☠ **Pharbitis** species/varieties, winder. Height: to 3 m (10 ft). Flowers white, pink, red, violet and blue; also possible striped, tricolor and double in early summer to early autumn. **Warning:** The entire plant is toxic!

☠ **Quamoclit** species, fast-growing winder. Height: to 3 m (10 ft). Yellow/orange/red flowers in mid summer to mid autumn. **Warning:** All parts are toxic!

☠ **Runner beans** (Phaseolus coccineus), fast-growing winding plant. Height: to 4 m (13 ft). Red flowers in early summer to mid autumn, fruit from mid summer. **Warning:** The beans are toxic when raw, but edible when cooked.

Scented sweet pea (Lathyrus odoratus). Height: to 2 m (7 ft). Scented flowers, white, yellow, pink and violet, mid summer to mid autumn.

Climbing plants create greenery on walls and a wealth of beautiful flowers in the smallest space. Many species only produce leaves in the summer and allow the sun to warm the housewall during the winter. Some of their other advantages are less well known: they filter road dust and dry out the foundations of walls. They also ensure an even temperature inside buildings, keeping them cool in summer and retaining heat in the winter. In addition, they offer a habitat for insects and birds. Climbing plants are even able to cover up any architectural shortcomings of buildings.

Climbing technique: The different species show their climbing skills in various ways. Most belong to the group of plants that wind up a support using the entire shoot. Others climb with the aid of sucker pads or use their leaf stalks to wind around supports. These plants require grid-shaped climbing aids. Plants with root suckers, like ivy (*Hedera helix*), are even able to climb across completely smooth surfaces without any aids. Never grow ivy on housewalls with damaged rendering, however, as it will grow into cracks and do further damage.

Ways to use climbing plants

They climb around lamps, posts and tree trunks.

They grow across arches.

They cover pergolas.

They grow all over ugly walls.

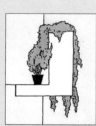

They hang down from balconies.

They frame steps in the garden.

They create a green façade. Many will require an espalier for this.

They cover up ugly drainpipes.

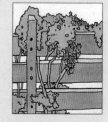

They creep over fences and disguise severe outlines.

Tips on designing

A skilful combination of perennials using poppies, foxgloves, geraniums and large daisies.

Perennials for every garden

Perennials are able to solve design problems in small gardens in surprising ways. They encourage experimentation. If a plant is not doing too well in one particular position, it can be moved in spring or autumn. It is important to consider the plant's requirements for soil and light when choosing plants. Also consider the height of growth, flowering time and colour of the flowers.

Solitary plants: Unusual perennials that grow to a great height, like *Eupatorium fistulosum* "Atropurpureum" (flower carmine red, mid summer to mid autumn), or *Rudbeckia lacinata* "Goldball" (yellow flower, late summer to early autumn) should have a position on their own so that they can show their full splendour. Such plants make an attractive eye-catching feature in a lawn or at the bend of a path.

Visual screens: Tall, autumn-flowering perennials, like the robust, rough-leafed *Aster novae-angliae* (flowers white, pink, red, violet, early to mid autumn) will provide a visual screen from the summer onwards if planted in rows.

Ground-cover plants: These are low-growing, spreading or cushion-shaped species that produce shoots or seed. Plant them in groups of about twenty to create greenery in spaces between shrubs, as an edging for paths or on slopes. Several species or varieties should be planted in groups in larger areas to avoid monotony. The following are suitable for sunny to semi-shady positions.

● *Astilbe chinensis* var. *pumila*, lilac pink flowers, late summer to early autumn.

● *Geranium macrorrhizum* "Spessart", whitish-pink flowers, late spring to mid summer.

● *Sedum floriferum* "Weihenstephaner Gold", yellow flowers, mid summer to early autumn.

Ground-cover plants for semi-shade and shade

● Barrenwort (*Epimedium pinnatum* ssp. *colchicum*), yellow flowers, mid to late spring.

● Blue-eyed Mary (*Omphalodes verna*), blue flower, early to late spring.

● Dead nettle (*Lamium galeobdolon "Florentinum"*), yellow flower, early to mid summer.

● Foam flower (*Tiarella cordifolia*), milk white flower, late spring to early summer.

● Greater periwinkle (*Vinca major*), light blue flowers, mid to late spring.

Large perennials for sunny and semi-sunny beds

Aster-dumosus hybrids, blue, violet, late summer to early autumn, 40 cm (16 in).
Autumn chrysanthemum (*Chrysanthemum indicum* hybrids), all colours except blue, early to late autumn, 60 cm (24 in).
Campanula (*Campanula persicifolia*), blue, white, early to late summer, 80 cm (32 in).
Christmas rose (*Helleborus niger "Praecox"*), white, mid autumn to early winter, 25 cm (10 in).
Delphinium hybrids, blue, white, pink, early summer to early autumn, 170 cm (68 in).
Gayfeather (*Liatris spicata*), violet, mid summer to early autumn, 80 cm (32 in).
Golden rod (*Solidago* hybrids), yellow, mid summer to early autumn, 80cm (32 in).
Helenium hybrids, yellow, copper, mid to late summer, 80 cm (32 in).
Iris (*Iris barbata* and *Iris spuria* hybrids), many colours, late spring to early

summer, 80 cm (32 in).
Leopard's bane (*Doronicum orientale*), yellow, mid to late spring, 40 cm (16 in).
Phlox (*Phlox paniculata*), white, pink, red, violet, early summer to early autumn, 50-150 cm (20-60 in).
Rudbeckia nitida "Herbstsonne", yellow, late summer to early autumn, 200 cm (80 in).
Rudbeckia fulgida "Goldsturm", yellow, late summer to early autumn, 70 cm (28 in).
Sedum telephium "Herbstfreude", rust red, late summer to mid autumn, 50 cm (20 in).
Shasta daisy (*Chrysanthemum maximum*) white, early summer to mid autumn, 60 cm (24 in).
Sunflower (*Helianthus decapetalus*), yellow, late summer to early autumn, 120 cm (48 in).
Yarrow (*Achillea filipendulina*), yellow, mid summer to early autumn, 120 cm (48 in).

Perennials for semi-shady to shady areas

Black snake-root (*Cimicifuga racemosa*), white, mid to late summer, 150 cm (60 in).
Campanula latifolia, blue, early to mid summer, 80 cm (32 in).
Hosta species, 20-100 cm (8-40 in).

Japanese anemone (*Anemone japonica* hybrids), white, pink, mid summer to mid autumn, 120 cm (48 in).
Male fern (*Dryopteris filix-mas*), 50-100 cm (20-40 in).

Plants with bulbs and tubers

The following can be left to grow wild:
Crocus species/hybrids, yellow, white, blue, early to late spring, 10 cm (4 in).
Narcissus species/hybrids, yellow, white, mid to late spring, 40 cm (16 in).
Scilla siberica, blue, early to mid spring, 20cm (8 in).
Snowdrop (*Galanthus nivalis*), white, late winter to early spring, 15 cm (6 in).
Winter aconite (*Eranthis hyemalis*), yellow, late winter to early spring, 10 cm (4 in).

To grow in beds:
Dahlia varieties, all colours except blue, mid summer to mid autumn, 30-160 cm (12-64 in).
Fritillary (*Fritillaria imperialis*), yellow, orange, mid to late spring, 80 cm (32 in).
Lilies (*Lilium* species/hybrids), many colours, early to mid summer, 100 cm (40 in).
Tulips (*Tulipa* species/hybrids), many colours, mid to late spring, 40 cm (16 in).

Tips on designing

Basic principles

The visual impression made by a bed depends mainly on how you combine tall and low-growing plants, together with attention to flowering times and colours.

Arranging heights: In the case of beds that will be viewed from all sides, the tallest plants should be planted in the centre and the shorter ones towards the edges. If the bed is in front of a boundary, plant the tallest plants at the back, the shortest at the front and medium-tall ones in between.

Flowering times: You will have to consider flowering times and the length of flowering when choosing plants if you want to have flowers all year round in your garden.

● Spring-flowering plants, like tulips and bleeding heart, will generally die back after flowering and leave unattractive gaps. These species are best planted in the centre or background of the bed.

● Early-summer-flowering types, like daisies, usually die back after flowering so the above advice applies to them as well.

● Summer-flowering plants will decorate a bed for weeks on end with their splendid colours. Place them in the bed according to height and colour distribution.

● Late-summer- and autumn-flowering-plants: Place low-growing ones, such as cushion-forming asters, in the foreground.

They will give visual stability to the bed. Taller species, such as autumn asters, should be planted in the middle and background.

Flower and leaf size: Both may influence the total effect of the garden. Small-flowered varieties planted in the background seem to push the boundary backwards, while large flowers appear to bring the boundary closer. The same rule applies to the size of the leaves.

Designing with colour

Disharmonious planting is much more noticeable in small gardens than in large ones. Before planting, make a plan showing the colours of simultaneously flowering plants and check that they complement each other. Also consider the colours in the immediate surroundings.

Strong colours look good in front of light-coloured walls. White and pastel-coloured flowers seem to glow in front of dark façades.

Colourful combinations look best in front of single-colour backgrounds.

Single colour plantings create tranquillity in front of an unrestful background.

Warm, fiery colours, such as red, orange and yellow, are eye-catching. If they are planted in the background, they appear to bring the boundary closer.

Cool colours, such as green and blue, seem more distant and elegant. Placed in the background, they appear to move the boundary back and this has the effect of enlarging the garden.

Plantings in several shades of the same colour require a certain amount of skill. Often only slight differences in shade will determine how a colour combination works. Standard combinations include: pink/violet; white/yellow; yellow/orange; red/red/white and pink/light blue/white.

Complementary colours are the three primary colours of red, yellow and blue, in each case combined with the colour made up of a mixture of the two other primary colours; i.e., red and green, yellow and violet and blue and orange. These combinations are eye-catching even from a distance.

Colour trios like yellow/red/blue or violet/orange/green always look harmonious, as do two partners from each of these trios. White flowers dampen disharmonious, rather daring combinations and will cause neighbouring, darker colours to glow.

This planting in many shades of the same colour takes into account the different shapes of the plants used.

Designing with shapes

In addition to the colours of flowers and leaves, the shape of growth will also determine the general picture created by every plant. Clumps of leaning plants can lessen the severe effect of a group of upright, single flowers. A uniform carpet of *Cerastium arvense*, on the other hand, will gain variety and tension from the upright flowers of tall lilies, for example. Further interesting contrasts are supplied by combinations of conspicuous flowers with simple ones, of large leaves with delicate ones, and of shiny surfaces with matt, felty ones.

Astilbe and roses, all in white.

An everlasting flowering bed

For your flowerbed, choose a particularly sunny position near a sitting area. If you like, you can choose a different main colour for every season (see p. 48). **My tip:** Build up your main bed step-by-step in the following sequence.

1 Trees and shrubs as focal points

(illustration 1)

The "frame" of the bed is formed by large shrubs or small trees. The best idea is to plant three woody species as anchors. Two taller ones, like yew, (*Taxus baccata*) (**toxic!**) and the yellow-flowering cornelian cherry (*Cornus mas*) should be placed in the background; low-growing woody species, such as bush roses (*Rosa* hybrids) in the central area. The shrubs should not be placed exactly symmetrically.

2 Making statements with taller perennials

(illustration 2)

Taller perennials are then placed in small groups between the framework bushes. Species that flower at about the same time should be combined and blended together according to their colours (see p. 48). Very vigorously growing plants, like white-flowering *Aruncus dioicus* with its huge green leaves, should be placed mainly in the background.

1 Trees and bushes as points of focus: a dark green yew, a yellow flowering cornelian cherry (Cornus mas) and a bush rose.

2 Make a point with tall plants. Imposing plants like white-flowering honeysuckle are set in small groups in the background.

3 Set shrubs that flower in the spring in the middle and background.

3 Spring-flowering plants
(illustration 3)

These species, like the yellow-flowering *Doronicum orientale* and the blue Caucasian forget-me-not (*Brunnera macrophylla*), die back after flowering and leave unattractive gaps. You should, therefore, place such plants in the middleground and background between plants that flower later so that the gaps can be quickly filled.

4 Early-summer-flowering plants
(illustration 4)

These plants should be placed in the background and middleground where the spring-flowering plants quietly die back in the summer. Blue violet *Aquilegia* hybrids and orange day lilies (*Hemerocallis* hybrids) were chosen for our planting example.

5 Summer- and autumn-flowering plants
(illustration 5)

Low-growing plants should be planted mainly in the foreground. From the summer onwards, lilac *Hosta* hybrids and pink autumn anemones (*Anemone japonica* hybrids) should be flowering. Autumn-flowering plants, like blue, cushion-forming asters, usually show lush green foliage all summer, as does *Festuca cinerea*. Taller summer and autumn-flowering plants should be placed mainly in the background (see p. 48).

6 Spring flowers with bulbs
(illustration 6)

Early-flowering bulbous plants, like tulips (*Tulipa* species/varieties), narcissus (*Narcissus* species/varieties) and many others, can be left to establish themselves undisturbed around woody plants and larger shrubs and allowed to go wild. Autumn is the planting time for these.

4 Early summer flowers. Blue lilac, aquilegia and orange day lilies will die back and should be placed in the middle and background.

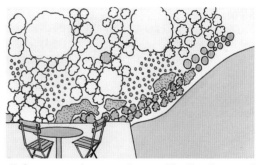

5 Summer and autumn flowers. The lilac flowers of hosta, blue cushions of aster and pink autumn anemones are set in the foreground.

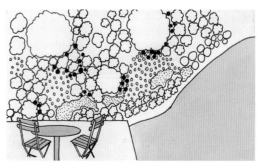

6 Spring flowers from bulbs planted around trees and bushes and between large perennials.

Tips on designing

Summer flowers

Annuals: After being sown in spring, these plants will flower only once, in the summer. Some species, like tagetes (*Tagetes* hybrids), flower tirelessly all summer long. Others, like love-in-a-mist (*Nigella damascena*) or summer larkspur *(Delphinium ajacis)*, flower early in the summer. Some, such as zinnia (*Zinnia elegans*) and *Cosmos bipinnatus*, flower from the second month of summer until the first frosts.

Balcony flowers: Many of these also flower from the last month of spring until the first frosts; for example, petunias (*Petunia* hybrids), pelargoniums (*Pelargonium* hybrids), fuchsias (*Fuchsia* hybrids), heliotrope (*Heliotropium arborescens*), *Lantana camara* hybrids and tuberous begonias (*Begonia* hybrids).

Biennial garden flowers: Sow these towards the end of the first month of summer in a special bed where they can overwinter undisturbed. After transplanting them in the following spring they will develop abundant flowers: (*Cheiranthus cheiri*), pansies (*Viola*-Wittrockiana hybrids), *Campanula medium* and snapdragon (*Antirrhinum majus*).

Colourful border plants

Low-growing cushion plants and prostrate perennials look graceful along the edges of paths. Good border plants are *Aubretia* hybrids, *Campanula cochleariifolia*, *Cerastium tomentosum*, pinks (*Dianthus gratianopolitanus*), candytuft (*Iberis sempervirens*), rock rose (*Helianthemum* hybrids), *Saxifraga* species and cushion phlox (*Phlox subulata*).

Beds framed by box hedges

Box edging along paths or around low-growing flower and vegetable beds creates an orderly design and gives the garden a hint of days gone by. If you have combined a great variety of plants in a slightly haphazard manner, this is one way to bring peace and order to the whole garden. The best box for edging, *Buxus sempervirens* "Suffruticosa", can be obtained at plant nurseries. Box can also be propagated quite easily at home, however. Cover some plants to half their height with soil in the autumn. The shoots will put out roots by spring. These can then be separated from the original plants and planted in a bed or in the position you want them.

Roses for every garden

For many people the rose is considered to be the queen of flowers for its scent and splendid blooms. In addition, because of its very variable shape of growth, it becomes possible to plant a rose in even the smallest garden. **NB:** Nearly all rose groups have specimens that flower continuously, twice or only once. Some varieties are particularly robust and will stay healthy even if they are not sprayed. Others regularly become infested with mildew, black spot or other diseases. If possible, choose robust varieties so that you do not need to use a spray too often.

Climbing roses are ideal for small gardens as they can be grown on an espalier without taking up much room.

Bush roses will complement a large bed but will also go with a hedge or can even be planted individually as an eye-catching feature.

Standards require only a small area of ground but need adequate winter protection.

Bedding roses look nice along paths and as a frame to beds. The multi-flowering Polyantha roses are better suited to small gardens than the large-flowered Floribunda roses. The latter will probably make the garden look even smaller.

Dwarf roses should find a space in even the smallest bed.

Ground-cover roses may be left to cover a slope with flowers and foliage.

Rambling roses usually only flower once, bear attractive hips and, when grown as hedges, will cover entire fences.

Companion plants for roses, such as summer-flowering plants with blue and white flowers or silvery grey foliage, will make the roses glow with colour. Delicate or spiky plants, such as grasses, will create a very elegant air. Try *Helicotrichon sempervirens*, *Festuca cinerea*, *Campanula carpatica*, catmint (*Nepeta* x *faassenii*), lavender (*Lavandula angustifolia*), sage (*Salvia nemorosa*), *Gypsophila paniculata* and *Veronica* species.

Roses combined with perennials, herbs and a box border.

A small, formal herb garden with box edging.

Tips on designing

A standard redcurrant with underplanting.

Strawberries growing in a pot on a pedestal.

Fruit in a small garden

Semi-standards or full standards are generally too large and broad for a small garden. More delicate shapes of fruit tree are more suitable for this situation.

Bushes: Apples, pears, peaches, acid cherry, apricot and quince are offered in this form. The stem will attain a height of about 60 cm (24 in).

Dwarf pyramid: This shape is found mainly in apple and pear. The stem is tied to a support post and will grow to 70 cm (28 in) tall. The crown will be more

slender than that of a bush. It is easy enough to learn how to prune into this shape.

Both types of shape have the advantage that care and harvesting can be done without the use of a ladder. The yield per bush, depending on the variety, will be 10-30 kg (20-60 lb).

Espalier: Fruit trees grown as espaliers will require very little space. This type of cultivation can also be used to provide other functions; for example, a property boundary, screen or partition in a garden.

NB: The position must be sunny!

Fruit in a large container:
Nearly all types of fruit can be grown in large containers. Such small trees naturally produce a smaller crop but they are quite enchanting when in flower.

Soft fruit

● Currants and gooseberries, depending on the variety, will need to be spaced 1.2-2 m (4-7 ft) apart. The standards, which need slightly more care, are particularly attractive and can be planted in flowerbeds.

Standards will require a support post that reaches right up into the crown.

A pocket amphora with alpine strawberries.

● Gooseberries are often susceptible to mildew so ask for the more resistant varieties.

● Raspberries require good soil. Here, too, virus-resistant varieties are now offered.

● Blackberries, with their long shoots, make an ideal visual screen and can substitute for a fence on a 1.8 m (6 ft) tall espalier. They require protection from frost in regions with severe weather. Varieties without thorns can be obtained but these need to be able to ripen properly to develop their full flavour.

● Grapes will flourish on sheltered, sunny walls even in areas outside the regular wine growing regions. Early and mildew-proof varieties are ideal for the garden.

Fruit with pips: Apples and pears must have another variety growing nearby for pollination purposes. Find out before purchasing whether other trees that would be able to pollinate your tree are already growing in the immediate vicinity. If this is not the case, you will have to plant at least two of the same species.

● A "family" fruit tree: This type of fruit tree has two different varieties grafted on to one stock so that they can pollinate each other. This would be ideal for a garden owner who does not have enough room for two trees.

My tip: Nowadays new apple cultivars have been created specially for growing in large containers. These "ballerina" and "minarette" varieties do not grow any higher than 1.5 m (5 ft). They do not form huge spreading crowns and bear fruit on short lateral shoots.

● Pear trees that do not grow very tall are also good for wall espaliers.

● A pear semi-standard with a final height of about 1.5 m (5 ft) is suitable as a main tree close to the house.

Fruit with stones: If you would like sweet cherries in your garden you should choose early varieties as they remain practically worm-free. However, pollination will only be ensured if other varieties of cherries also grow in the vicinity.

NB: Sweet cherries grow relatively tall. Even varieties that do not grow very fast attain heights of 3 m (10 ft).

Acid cherries (*Prunus cerasus*) come in dwarf varieties. Medium-slow-growing varieties can be obtained of acid cherries, peaches, apricots and plums. Properly pruned, their height can be limited to about 3 m (10 ft). Most varieties do not require a partner for pollination.

Tips on designing

A raised bed of herbs and vegetables.

The vegetable plot

Vegetables require full sunlight so do not place your beds in the shadow of trees or bushes or failure will be programmed in right from the start. A few square metres will be sufficient to supply your kitchen with fresh vegetables and herbs. If you plan and plant with forethought, you will be able to plant and harvest each bed two to three times in succession.

Design tips

● Try looking upon vegetables as ornamental plants that can be combined attractively colourwise. There is a large range of red-leafed lettuces or blue cabbage varieties that look attractive with green-leafed vegetables.

● Plant flowers in between vegetables; for example, marigolds which have a beneficial effect on the soil and also provide interesting yellow and orange accents. Many herbs, such as dill or borage, have enchanting flowers.

● Experimenting with rare vegetable species like sweet corn, mangolds, broad beans and sugarbeet, or with unusual varieties like yellow or plum tomatoes, purple peppers or white cucumbers can be a fascinating pastime.

Pale pink beetroots are popular in households with small children.

Strawberries: Most varieties have to be replaced every three to four years and planted in a fresh bed. The longlasting, ground-cover varieties "Spadeka" and "Florika" are easy to care for and can be used to create a "strawberry field" on a few square metres of ground. The following alternatives can also be planted in small gardens.

● The small alpine strawberries flower and bear fruit from the last month of spring until the second month of autumn and produce no runners so they do not need much room.

● Climbing strawberries form shoots up to 1.5 m (5 ft) long and can be grown in large containers just like tomatoes and also in a bed where they take up very little room. Simply drive in a firm support next to the plant and gradually tie the shoots to the support. These strawberry plants will also yield lots of fruit when grown in hanging baskets.

Cultivation in large containers

Herbs and vegetables can be grown in decorative containers. They create a pleasant picture on the patio or in front of a window.

Mini-ponds in tubs and troughs

If there is not enough space for a pond, decorative wooden tubs or concrete rings containing a liner and a few water plants can always be accommodated in a small corner. The position needs plenty of sunlight. Small baskets or pots of marginal plants can be set just under the surface of the water or placed on a plinth or platform made of bricks. Plant this area sparingly rather than abundantly as water and marginal plants tend to grow extremely vigorously. Emphasize the surroundings of a mini-pond with perennials whose growth is reminiscent of marginal plants, such as bamboo, grasses, *Bergenia*, lady's mantle, irises, day lilies or *Hosta.*

Compost: Do not use garden soil for water and marginal plants. Instead, use nutrient-poor, sandy-loamy subsoil or special water plant compost from the gardening trade. A high nutrient content will only encourage the growth of algae.

Water: Naturally, rainwater is best. Chlorinated mains water should be allowed to stand for a few days before planting in it. As far as possible, do not change the water again later on. Top up water lost through evaporation with rainwater.

Care: In the beginning algae and floating plants will tend to flourish. Remove them regularly in the same way as falling leaves. This will slowly decrease the nutrient content of the water and it will become clearer. Water plants that grow too vigorously should be cut back from time to time. This mini-pond can be kept in a cool room during the winter or else bury it in soil to protect it from frost and cover it with a plank.

Wildlife: In time, mini-ponds will be colonized by dragonflies, pond skaters and common backswimmers. The latter will also consume unwanted creatures such as mosquito larvae. Water snails will graze on carpets of algae. You should not keep fish in mini-ponds.

Security: Even small basins are a danger to young children and a mini-pond should not be accessible to them. Children should not be allowed to play in their vicinity without supervision. A small piece of wood set diagonally into the water and fixed into position will enable small creatures (hedgehogs, bees) to climb out of the pond if they fall in.

Tips on designing

By moving plants in containers, colour can be created in different places at any time of the year.

A mobile garden

Many plants will flourish in decorative large containers. There are several advantages to containers.

● You can move features about.

● You can change the planting depending on the time of year.

Position: Large container plants will be comfortable wherever there is sufficient light; for example, on a patio, in front of an entrance door, along reinforced paths, in gardens or small courtyards, in niches, in front of a housewall or windows or on balconies.

Plants: In addition to the usual large container plants, you can use balcony plants, garden flowers, herbs, vegetables or fruit or even evergreen woody species like box and dwarf conifers. Plants in hanging containers are also very attractive.

Overwintering: Most large container plants require a cool, bright position.

Index

Index

Author's notes

This volume is concerned with the design and building of small gardens. Please visit a doctor as soon as possible if you receive an injury while handling soil or while building garden elements, to discuss the possibility of having a tetanus vaccination. If you are planning to build a pond and also have small children you should surround the pond with a protective fence or use a surface grid. Every pond owner must also ensure that no water – either above or below ground – can flow on to a neighbour's property. Remember that electrical installations should only be carried out by an expert. Lethally toxic plants, and even less toxic ones that may cause health problems in susceptible adults or children, are marked with a warning symbol on pages 34-35, 44 and 47 in the plant tables and emphasized as such in the text. Make absolutely sure that children and domestic pets do not eat plants indicated as being toxic.

All fertilizers and plant protection agents, even organic ones, should be stored in such a way that they are inaccessible to children and domestic pets. Consumption of these substances may result in damage to health. Do not allow such substances to come into contact with the eyes.

June flowers along a fence

Seemingly grown at random, these tall perennials are grouped in a corner of the garden where they cleverly disguise the wire mesh fence and simultaneously create a charming visual screen. If you decide to hide a problem in this way, stagger the plants according to height by placing the tallest at the back followed by increasingly shorter ones towards the front. In this way, the ensemble will gain depth and the eye of the observer is gradually led upwards from flower to flower.

White valerian, yellow green lady's mantle and blue delphiniums. The pink hybrid lilies in the centre carry the eye back to the foxglove, lupins and climbing rose.

Cover photographs

Front cover: *Splendid shrubs and roses border a path.*
Inside front cover: *A small front garden filled with cottage garden plants.*
Back cover: *Add colour in your garden with large container plants and summer flowers in pots.*

Photographic acknowledgements

Becker: front cover, 5 right, 7, 12 top, bottom, 22, 27 top, bottom, 40 left, right, 46, 49 top, bottom, 53 top, bottom, 56, back cover;
Nickig: p. 2, 3 left, right, 28/29, 29 right;
Schlaback-Becker: p. 41;
Schneiders, T: p. 4/5;
Schneiders, U: inside front cover/1, 10, 14/15, 15 right, 38/39, 39 right, 58, 62/63;
Strauss: p. 32, 54 left, right, 55.

This edition published 1996 by Merehurst Limited
Ferry House, 51-57 Lacy Road, Putney, London SW15 1PR

© 1995 Gräfe und Unzer GmbH, Munich

ISBN 1 85391 559 9

A catalogue record for this book is available from the British Library.

English text copyright © Merehurst Limited 1996
Translated by Astrid Mick
Edited by Lesley Young
Design and typesetting by Paul Cooper Design
Printed in Hong Kong by Wing King Tong

Other titles available in the series

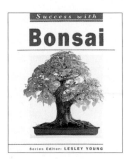

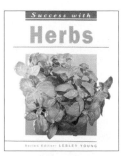

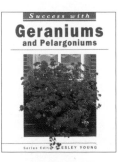

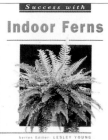